HUMMINGBIRDS

HUMMINGBIRDS

Photographs by
Tony Keppelman

•

Foreword by
Roger Tory Peterson

A NEW YORK GRAPHIC SOCIETY BOOK
LITTLE, BROWN AND COMPANY • BOSTON

To my mother and father

FIRST EDITION

The publisher is grateful for permission to include the following previously copyrighted
material:

"Mirrorment" is reprinted from *Collected Poems 1951–1971* by A. R. Ammons, by
permission of W. W. Norton and Company, Inc. Copyright © 1972 by A. R. Ammons.

Excerpt from "Here All Beautifully Collides" by Ray Bradbury. Copyright © 1976 by
Ray Bradbury. Reprinted by permission of Don Congdon Associates, Inc., from *When
Elephants Last in the Dooryard Bloomed* by Ray Bradbury (Alfred A. Knopf, Inc.).

Excerpt from "i/never" by e.e. cummings. Copyright © 1963 by Marion Morehouse
Cummings. Reprinted from *Complete Poems 1913–1962* by E.E. Cummings, by
permission of Harcourt Brace Jovanovich, Inc., and Grafton Books–A Division of the
Collins Publishing Group.

Excerpt from poem number 1463 by Emily Dickinson. Reprinted from *The Complete
Poems of Emily Dickinson,* edited by Thomas H. Johnson (Little, Brown and
Company, Inc., 1960).

Excerpt from "Humming-Bird" in *The Complete Poems of D. H. Lawrence,* collected
and edited by Vivian de Sola Pinto and F. Warren Roberts. Copyright © 1964, 1971
by Angelo Ravagli and C. M. Weekley, Executors of the Estate of Frieda Lawrence
Ravagli. All rights reserved. Reprinted by permission of Viking Penguin Inc., Lawrence
Pollinger Ltd., and the Estate of Mrs. Frieda Lawrence Ravagli.

Excerpt from "Hummingbird" in *Stone, Paper, Knife* by Marge Piercy.
Copyright © 1983 by Marge Piercy. Reprinted by permission of Alfred A. Knopf, Inc.

Library of Congress Cataloging-in-Publication Data

Keppelman, Tony.
  Hummingbirds.

  "A New York Graphic Society book."
  1. Hummingbirds — Pictorial works.   2. Photography
of birds.   3. Birds — Pictorial works.   I. Title.
QL696.A558K47   1988   598.9′99   87-29684
ISBN 0-8212-1617-1

New York Graphic Society books are published by
Little, Brown and Company (Inc.)

Published simultaneously in Canada by
Little, Brown & Company (Canada) Limited

PRINTED IN JAPAN

Contents

•

Foreword

●

Roger Tory Peterson

When Professor Harold Edgerton of MIT developed the first stroboscopic lights in the early 1930s, among his first subjects were Ruby-throated Hummingbirds, which he photographed at the feeders on Mrs. Lawrence Webster's piazza in Holderness, New Hampshire. This was even before he published his famous pictures of bullets passing through objects and of drops of water and milk splashing into a saucer.

Because of the high speed of their wing motion, too fast for our eyes, hummingbirds have been a perennial favorite with technicians who are fascinated by birds and high-tech photography. Now that one can buy a modest strobe of sorts at any camera store, I have tried my own luck with hummingbirds at Madera Canyon in the Santa Ritas, the Mile High in the Huachucas, Cave Creek Canyon in the Chiricahuas, and other hot spots in the mountains of southeastern Arizona, where hummingbird feeders proliferate and a dozen species of hummers might be expected. By contrast, at my home in Connecticut we have only one species, the Ruby-throated, and seldom more than one individual, which neglects the feeder in favor of the cardinal flowers and salvias in the butterfly garden that my wife, Ginny, has planted.

I must confess that my pictures taken in Arizona with a simple strobe have always been disappointing; they suffer badly in comparison with the work of those sophisticates who have followed in the wake of Professor Edgerton, using literally vanloads of equipment. I am an artist by training, a visual person, defeated by the intricacies of high technology.

It fell to Crawford Greenwalt to publish the first extensive photographic treatise on hummingbirds, in 1960. It was not a handbook or guide to every species of Trochilidae (343 have been identified so far, all of them in the New World, mostly in the tropics). The classic work of that sort had been published a hundred years earlier by John Gould of England, who between 1849 and 1861 produced a massive, five-volume series illustrated with Audubon-like, full-page colored lithographs of each species known at that time.

However, Greenwalt's book was the first photographic presentation to treat hummingbirds in depth. It emphasized their physical attributes: what makes them different from other birds and, especially, the mechanics of their incredibly fast wing action and the physical properties of their iridescent colors. Drawing upon the resources of his associates at Dupont, Greenwalt devised special high-speed flash equipment. With this apparatus he documented a representative selection of hummers — some from the southwestern United States, others from the American tropics.

More recently, Esther and Robert Tyrrell produced a dazzling portfolio and text covering the sixteen species that normally breed in the contiguous United States. Robert Tyrrell documented everything from nidification to molt with his microsharp photography, while his wife, Esther, prepared a scholarly text that tells us everything we need to know about these fragile birds — their anatomy, food, metabolism, courtship, nesting, migration, ecology, and even their symbiotic parasites.

In this new book, Tony Keppelman offers us a feast of his own superb photographs, most of them taken in the same southwestern canyons where Greenwalt and the Tyrrells worked. But whereas his predecessors presented the basic facts about hummers and their habits, he has taken a different tack, emphasizing another dimension: the unbelievable spirit and vitality of these feathered mites. Small and energy-packed, their wings a blur when they come in to feed, hummers place their needlelike bills with precision into the throats of flowers and then back away in a manner unique among birds. They are, indeed, a very vivid expression of life. Like butterflies, they suggest flying flowers, but with the addition of gemlike iridescence made possible by the structure of their feathers.

It is this quality of spirit and intense energy that intrigues Keppelman and that he sees as an affirmation at the very root of life itself. To use his words, hummingbirds express vividly in their action-packed lives something that is "timeless and eternal" in all living things.

Study these photographs as state-of-the-art examples of strobe photography; but also enjoy them as evocative images of our most unbirdlike birds. And then plan to visit, if you can, some of the canyons in southeastern Arizona that have become so famous among hummingbird aficionados.

Introduction

●

I set out to photograph hummingbirds as well as or better than they had been photographed. For me this meant creating a high-resolution photograph with accurate color and very little grain — one in which the bird was so frozen in flight that I could see every detail of the wings and feathers. I wanted an even, neutral, light background, something that would not detract from the form of the bird or from the delicacy of detail in its finest parts.

At the time, I saw the photographing of these birds in technical terms. I was not aware of the deeper aspects of what I was doing. I discovered this later, when the first transparencies came back and I saw the pictures. Even then I only barely realized it. It was not until still later, when I made the big, 16×20-inch enlargements, that I really began to see what I had accomplished. And the realization continued to unfold as I showed the prints and as I listened to what I was saying about them. Then, too, there were people who saw things of which I was not aware. Each presentation brought forth new information.

Through all of this I realized that what had started out as a technical challenge had evolved into far more. I had, through the clarity and detail I had achieved, gone far more deeply into seeing the bird than I had set out to do. I saw in these photographs the amazing strength and brilliance of life's energy — the spirit.

And so these photographs are about the spirit of these little birds, and through them about spirit itself. I see in them an affirmation of what I consider to be at the very root of life. I will not go into a long discussion of what I feel spirit is; let it suffice to say that it is that which is timeless and eternal in all of us and in all of life. That which connects all of us to each other and to everything we experience. It is the common denominator, the essence of life — pure, timeless, eternal energy.

The whole attitude of the hummingbird embodies this energy. There is a supernatural quality to the purity and intensity that these birds project. I see it in practically all facets of their existence. Take, for instance, the migration of the Ruby-throated. Every year it flies thousands of miles — from Central America to southern Canada and back — including a five-hundred-mile solo stretch across the Gulf of Mexico without food or rest. At a cruising speed of twenty-five miles per hour, that is twenty hours of nonstop flight. The Rufous flies round-trip from Mexico to Alaska every year, an even longer journey — nearly three thousand miles each way, many of them out over the Pacific. Each of these two birds weighs only about three grams, which is less than the weight of two dimes.

Then there is the way these birds fly. Because they can pivot or pitch their wings at the body, they are able to fly straight up or down or backward, or hover stationary in the air, all while facing forward, and they can switch between these various modes of flight in any order. No other bird can do this. They can even fly upside down. And because of their ability to pitch their wings, hummers can also start and stop quickly. They beat their wings at full speed, then simply by changing the angle of the wing immediately take off. The 3½-inch-long birds can go from cruising speed to zero in the space of five inches. They can also dive at speeds of more than eighty-five miles an hour. The list goes on.

Hummingbirds are restricted entirely to the New World. Within the family of 343 species is the smallest bird in the world — in fact, the smallest warm-blooded creature: the Bee Hummingbird of Cuba is a mere 2¼ inches long. Many hummers are tiny, but not all. The largest, the Giant Hummingbird of western South America, is 8½ inches long. The wingbeats of the bigger birds are slower than those of the smaller ones. The wings of 3½-inch hummingbirds, including most of the hummers found in the United States, beat eighty times per second during hovering. (One beat equals a full cycle from the top of the wing sweep to the bottom and back up to the top again.)

The diet of the hummingbird consists of very small flies and nectar from flowers and feeders. They eat up to five times their weight each day. The feathers of their gorgets (the shiny throat) reflect more brilliance of color and light than those of any other bird. Beautifully designed, these tight-fitting, platelike mirrors are extremely smooth and provide almost no measurable air resistance. This quality of low air resistance is true of the whole body. It is difficult to describe how the beak, head, and body flow together to make such a highly efficient, aerodynamic shape, but it is easy to see in the photographs. The transition from beak to body is remarkably graceful. The feathers are smooth and flat, and the feet tuck up inside when the bird is in full flight, allowing it to slip effortlessly through the air. Even in sleep the hummingbird is astounding. It can slow its heartbeat almost to the point of death, thereby allowing itself the deepest of rests.

These are but a few of the amazing facts about these extraordinary birds. And the photographs will show you more than I can tell. You will see their jewel-like brilliance, the power in their wings, their incredible energy, and the grace of the whole of them. These are the birds of the gods, the dancers of the air.

Acknowledgments

•

I would like to give my deepest thanks to the people listed below,
without whose help this book would not have happened.

Elizabeth and Phillips Finlay
Diana Kappel-Smith
Del Keppelman
Jim Meagher
Paul Smith
Bill Mayer
Betty Douglas
Joan and Carroll Peabody
Crawford Greenwald

HUMMINGBIRDS

A Route of Evanescence
With a revolving Wheel —
A Resonance of Emerald —
A Rush of Cochineal. . . .

— Emily Dickinson

•

Plate 1

Plate 2

Plate 3

Plate 4

Plate 5

Plate 6

Plate 7

Plate 8

Plate 9

Before anything had a soul,
While life was a heave of Matter, half inanimate,
This little bit chipped off in brilliance
And went whizzing through the slow, vast, succulent stems.

I believe there were no flowers then,
In the world where the humming-bird flashed ahead of creation.

    — D. H. Lawrence

Plate 10

Plate 11

Plate 12

*Birds are flowers flying
and flowers perched birds.*

— A. R. Ammons

Plate 13

Plate 14

Plate 15

Plate 16

Plate 17

Plate 18

Plate 19

Metallic apparition whirring
like a helicopter,
the golden nightingale of the Chinese
emperor breaking the sound
barrier, you seem almost
a weapon, too exquisite,
too expensive to be
useful, flashing
like a jeweled signal. . . .

— Marge Piercy

Plate 20

Plate 21

Plate 22

Plate 23

Plate 24

Plate 25

i
never
guessed any
thing(even a
universe)might be
so not quite believab
ly smallest as perfect this
(almost invisible where of a there of a)here of a
rubythroat's home. . . .

— e. e. cummings

Plate 26

Plate 27

Plate 28

Here all beautifully collides
Unfrictioned;
Summer heals all with an oiled and motioned ease.
Here no disease.
Here health of world in distilled proportion,
Here gyroscope ahum kept spun by bees
Who drowse-drawn lusciously entrapped by flowers
Or hummingbirds which fatten forth the hours with pure dripped sound. . . .

— Ray Bradbury

Plate 29

Plate 30

Plate 31

Plate 32

Plate 33

Epilogue

This study started out as a job for a book in progress on hummingbirds. I researched what had already been done and decided that my approach would be to show the birds fully frozen in flight without anything else in the picture. This way they could really be seen as you normally never see them. But this posed some technical problems: Somehow the birds had to be carefully focused and centered in the frame of the camera. The photographs had to be made at very high speed to stop all of the wing motion. And the branches, flowers, feeders, bees, and so on had to be eliminated from the camera's view.

I had the idea to devise a light beam that the bird would fly through on its way to a feeder. The camera would be carefully focused on this beam, and when the bird entered it, the shutter would be automatically triggered and the bird would be photographed in focus and in the middle of the frame. The trick was to design such a beam and marry it to my motorized camera so that the whole thing would work fast enough to catch the bird in flight.

Then there was the problem of stopping the wings. No camera shutter is fast enough, but a strobe light can be made to be. I had a very old but very powerful strobe unit, and I took this and my idea to my friend Jim Meagher and his co-worker Paul Smith, both electrical engineers. The three of us, mostly they, designed and built the light beam and rewired the strobe so it would be fast enough.

The last problem was elimination of anything but the birds. For this I hung a piece of neutral, light-colored mount board as a background just behind the feeder. This also helped to lighten the area around the bird. Because the strobe lights are so bright in relation to the ambient daylight, the birds would appear in the photographs to be flying in the dark unless there was something close behind them to reflect light back to the camera. I could control the brightness of this background by moving the board toward or away from the strobes.

I took these tools along with many more into the field and began learning how to photograph the hummer. It took me two months of experimenting before I got what I wanted. I learned that by changing the distance and angle of the light beam in relation to the feeder, I could get many different points of view of the birds. With the beam five inches away from the feeder, I got shots of them in full flight. At four inches, I got them braking; at three inches, hovering. Then, by changing the angle of the beam and feeder in relation to the camera, I could get a view of them flying straight toward the camera, or a full side view, or anything in between. I took careful notes and practiced with black-and-white film, which I developed right on the spot to check my results.

At the end of the two months, I was ready to work seriously. My close friend Bill Mayer, a poet, writer, and birder, was doing the work of researching where we should go to find the species we needed. I was in charge of all the technical aspects, including wiring the car for 110 volts to run the strobe unit. I built a platform on the roof for sleeping, as we knew we would be camping and it is dangerous to sleep on the desert floor (snakes, spiders, and scorpions like to crawl into your sleeping bag for moisture).

Bill had found a place in southeastern Arizona, way up in the Huachuca Mountains, called the Mile High — a birders' resort — and that is where we headed. The Violet-crowned Hummingbird, which was the species we were looking for in particular, had been seen often there, so we left the coast of California in our heavily equipped little Volvo. Bill writes about our experience in the Afterword.

Afterword

•

Bill Mayer

The best time for photographing was the early morning, just before sunrise. Late afternoon to dusk was nearly as good, but the days were simply too hot. We would get up with the light gray, hurriedly throw our things into the car, and leave the campsite (usually little more than a pullout on a dirt road). Setting up the elaborate equipment quickly, we could expect to begin work by six A.M. By this time the birds were coming so thickly that the sound of their wings and constant chattering were all you could hear. The big canyon sycamores kept the cool in as we sat, some fifteen feet from the feeder, watching carefully as they came. It was tricky and tiring because they came and left so fast and we only wanted pictures of certain species. We would work steadily for four to five hours, then stop and wait for the cooler evenings to bring the birds back.

The desert country of southeastern Arizona is fairly high, broken by several short, ragged mountain ranges. Like most deserts, there is very little rain, but the mountains, unexpectedly, get much more. The vegetation between five thousand and seven thousand feet is actually rather lush, even semitropical in places. To these areas hummingbirds, some of which generally migrate only within Mexico, come in late spring. There is not another area like it farther north and you must go several hundred miles south to find anything similar. These regions are like tiny islands at the extreme north end of the range of several species of hummingbirds. The Violet-crowned, photographed herein, is an especially good example. Probably only a handful of individuals cross the border each year; most summer in the rugged, tropical mountains between Durango and Mazatlán, nearly seven hundred miles to the south. How or why a few of them continue all the way to the United States is a mystery.

But they and other species do come, giving southeastern Arizona the largest number of species seen in the country. In Ramsey Canyon alone, every species in this country has been sighted with the odd exception of the Ruby-throated, the common hummingbird of the eastern United States and Canada.

There are three mountain areas in the Southwest that are especially attractive to hummingbirds: the Santa Ritas, the Chiricahuas, and the Huachucas — particularly the latter, in the north-facing canyons, perhaps fifteen miles from the Mexican border. At the Mile High ranch in Ramsey Canyon, a resort geared to bird-watchers, hummingbird feeders are constantly maintained, filled up to four times each day. At peak hours there are so many birds it seems positively dangerous to walk across the lawns. But there never seem to be any collisions, the birds' miraculous maneuverability preventing any mishap. While working there, we counted eleven different species. Later, we moved to the Chiricahua Mountains and worked near Cave Creek Canyon and the Southwestern Research Station, where we came upon several students experimenting with different-colored feeders to see which the hummingbirds preferred. They had a choice of green, yellow, blue, and red. That day at least, red was the drink of choice.

We worked directly out of the small Volvo. All equipment, including several cameras, ten tripods, three flash units, power boxes, wires, remote-control and light-sensor devices (plus duplicates), as well as a box of odds and ends, fitted neatly, or at least fitted, into the car. Add to this personal belongings, an ice chest for the film, pots, a Coleman stove, sleeping bags, maps and hummingbird literature, a little food, and you might understand how we were a bit cramped for space.

In June, Arizona temperatures often stay above 100 degrees Fahrenheit until midnight. This posed a constant problem, for color film must be kept reasonably cool; otherwise the color "shifts." Not only does the film need to be stored during the day in an ice chest, but it also must be protected from heat during the actual shooting. We were forced to shade the camera constantly, hoping we could get our shots quickly enough and then rush the film back to the cooler. At times, people kindly lent us a corner of their refrigerator, as ice was not always easy to come by. When sending the film to Kodak for processing, we had to make sure that it was kept cool in transit. Sometimes that meant constantly checking various mailboxes, or else waiting for the mail truck, all the while hoping that the truck itself would not be too hot, or the transit too long.

The worst problems occurred when the equipment malfunctioned. At times the synchronization was off; we would hear the click of the shutter and then see the flash, or else the reverse. Tinkering, cross-checking, we were kept busy and frustrated for days. Once, we had to leave our site, drive back to Tucson, and send the camera by air to San Francisco, then wait, impatiently, for its return several days later.

When we visited, southern Arizona had been afflicted by a serious drought for over a year. All National Forest land had been closed because the fire danger was so great. The stream in Ramsey Canyon, which usually flows all year, was dry and had been for quite some time. The ferns and vines were brown and the great sycamores and other riparian trees were drooping. In the Chiricahuas, we watched lightning start six small fires and heard of many more. Unfortunately, the turbulence produced far more thunder than it did showers.

The conditions prevented our going farther up the canyons and into the mountains. Most of the hummingbirds we wanted to photograph had arrived, however, even if in smaller numbers than usual. There were certainly enough to keep us occupied.

The seven species photographed herein vary in size from tiny — under 3 inches from tip of beak to end of tail — to large (for hummers), over 5 inches. It should be mentioned here that the physical descriptions below pertain to the male of the species only. The female is drab, usually green-backed and pale underneath, with little or no iridescence. Although the female and the male of a particular species are roughly identical in size and general body shape, females of different species are often virtually indistinguishable from one another in the field. It is easy to tell a female Blue-throated (a 5-inch bird) from a female Black-chinned (a 3½-inch bird), for instance; but it is not so easy to tell a female Broad-tailed from a female Ruby-throated (both are about 3½ inches long). To further complicate matters, immature males look like the females.

Perhaps the most common hummer in the mountains in June was the Black-chinned. A small, svelte hummingbird with a lovely white collar and "black chin" — which at the right angle reveals itself to be a rich blue-violet — it is surprisingly difficult to photograph. This is due in part to the smallness of the gorget area that has color; the upper portion, the chin, has no iridescence. It is the common hummer of the Southwest, occasionally seen as far north as Canada. It prefers desert and semiarid country. Its chattering and bickering were the dominant noises surrounding our work. Very aggressive and curious, Black-chinned Hummingbirds on several occasions flew up to hover a foot or so in front of our eyes, evaluating what manner of creatures we might be.

Broad-tailed Hummingbirds were also fairly common. It is easy to prepare for them because you can hear them well before they come to the feeder. Owing to a peculiar fluting of the wing tips, these birds make an unmistakable shrill, metallic trill as they fly.

In early morning and just before dark, the feeders were dominated by the two large hummers of the area: the Rivoli (Magnificent) and the Blue-throated. Both are nearly twice the weight of a Black-chinned, and the Blue-throated is the largest hummer in the country. Their wings move more slowly than those of the Black-chinned; you can actually see them as the birds hover at the feeder. Of the two, Rivoli is really the more stunning. From a distance, perched, he appears slender, all black with a brilliant white eye. The effect of his swooping nearby is dazzling and a little uncanny. The entire body seems iridescent, black suddenly blooming into an almost painfully brilliant green. Beside him, the Blue-throated appears plain, especially the female. But the great size of the Blue-throated, comparatively speaking — larger than many wrens, finches, and titmice — can be almost shocking. The Blue-throated was the only bird we saw actually muscle his way to the feeder among the Broad-tailed and tiny Black-chinned hummers.

Another bird, similar in range, is the Broad-billed. This hummer looks distinctly tropical; the bill is, as its name suggests, wide at the base, and is bright orange; the throat is a brilliant, rich blue; and the rest of him, a deep green. In certain lights he was absolutely beautiful.

The rarest bird we photographed was the Violet-crowned. In all likelihood we saw and photographed the only individual that had made the long journey from Mexico to Arizona that summer. In any event, we were near the end of our stay when he unexpectedly appeared at the feeder. Pure white underneath, he displayed an orange bill and violet crown that made him look almost regal. The Violet-crowned is a little larger than most hummers (though considerably smaller than the Rivoli), and flies differently — quietly and directly. He always turned up unexpectedly; there was no way to prepare for him. All of a sudden he simply would be there, quietly hovering, and then was gone, like an apparition. We had to be constantly alert, because there were only a few chances to get his picture.

If you live in the eastern United States, you are probably quite familiar with the Ruby-throated, a common visitor as far north as Canada. It is the only hummingbird ever seen east of the Mississippi River. Utterly fearless and remarkably strong, it is a migrator of prodigious distances. Its brilliant red gorget makes it unmistakable.

The Ruby-throated was photographed at Brown Tract Pond in the Adirondack Mountains of New York. Much more patience was required for these photographs than for those taken in the Southwest, simply because there were fewer individuals at the site chosen. And before any pictures were taken, it was always necessary to establish a feeding area that the birds would return to over and over again each day. Nonetheless, the hummingbirds' behavior remained constant, in New York and in Arizona. Once we set up, no matter where we were working, it was always reassuring to find them just as curious, just as fearless, and just as photogenic.

Plates

•

Edited by Ray A. Roberts and Robin Jacobson

Designed by Nelida Nassar

Production coordinated by Christina M. Holz

Typeset by Cool-Comp, Inc.

Separated, printed, and bound by Dai Nippon Printing Company, Ltd.